D1028949

Welcome to Italy

By Mary Berendes

The Child's World®

Welcome to the WORLD

Published by The Child's World®
1980 Lookout Drive
Mankato, MN 56003-1705
800-599-READ
www.childsworld.com

Content Adviser: Professor Gichana C. Manyara,
Department of Geography, Radford University, Radford, VA
Design and Production: The Creative Spark, San Juan Capistrano, CA
Editorial: Emily J. Dolbear, Brookline, MA
Photo Research: Deborah Goodsite, Califon, NJ

Cover and title page: David Woolley/Taxi/Getty Images
Interior photos: Alamy: 11 (Visual Arts Library (London)), 15 (Sam Bloomberg-Rissman/David
Sanger Photography), 25 (Peter Horree); Animals Animals—Earth Scenes: 8 (ROGER DE LA HARPE);
Bruce Coleman Inc.: 19 (Danilo Donadoni); Corbis: 12 (Bettmann), 18 (John Heseltine); iStockphoto.com:
21 (Norma Cornes), 22 (gaffera), 28 (Ufuk Zivana), 30 (Tina Lorien), 31 (Hedda Gjerpen); John
Warburton-Lee Photography: 26 (Christian Kober); Lonely Planet Images: 3, 24 (Eoin Clarke); Minden
Pictures: 3, 9 (KONRAD WOTHE); NASA Earth Observatory: 4 (Reto Stockli); Oxford Scientific: 6
(J-C&D. Pratt/Photononstop), 7 (Olivier Grunewald), 17 (Michael Newton/Robert Harding Picture
Library Ltd), 23 (Sue Darlow), 3, 27 (Bruno Morandi/Robert Harding Picture Library Ltd), 29 (Laura
Wagner/Index Stock Imagery); Photo Researchers, Inc.: 13 (Gianni Tortoli), 14 (David R. Frazier), 16
(Ameller/Explorer), 20 (Pasquale Sorrentino); SuperStock: 10 (Philip & Karen Smith).
Map: XNR Productions: 5

Library of Congress Cataloging-in-Publication Data
Berendes, Mary.
  Welcome to Italy / by Mary Berendes.
      p. cm. — (Welcome to the world)
  Includes index.
  ISBN-13: 978-1-59296-918-0 (library bound : alk. paper)
  ISBN-10: 1-59296-918-6 (library bound : alk. paper)
  1. Italy—Juvenile literature. I. Title. II. Series.

DG417.B474 2007
945—dc22

                                          2007005556

Contents

Where Is Italy?

Earth is a colorful place from far away. You can see blues, reds, browns, greens, and whites. The huge blue areas are Earth's oceans, and the white wisps are clouds. The big brown patches are land areas called continents. Italy is a country on the continent of Europe. Many people say the country of Italy is shaped like a boot!

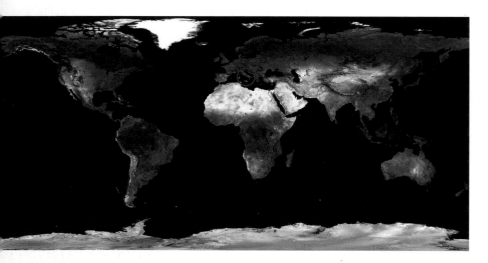

This picture gives us a flat look at Earth. Italy is inside the red circle.

Did you know?

There are two small independent nations in Italy. They are Vatican City in Rome and the **Republic** of San Marino.

4

The Land

Italy is a **peninsula**. A peninsula is a piece of land surrounded by water on almost all sides. On the Italian peninsula, there are many different types of landscapes. There are thick forests and large, flat areas of land called **plains**. There are sandy beaches, deep valleys, and steep cliffs. There are also stunning mountains in Italy. The snowy Alps are in the north. Farther south are the Apennines.

The Italian Alps

Italy has two major islands—Sicily and Sardinia. Sicily has mountains, plains, and a volcano called Mount Etna. Sardinia is covered mostly by hills and mountains.

Mount Etna is the highest active volcano in Europe.

Grapes growing in Tuscany

Plants and Animals

Because Italy has so many kinds of land, it has many kinds of plants, too. Oak and evergreen trees are in the deep forests of the Alps. Short bushes and grasses grow in lower areas. Italy's warm weather also helps olive and grape plants grow.

Many kinds of animals make their homes in Italy. Bears, foxes, and wolves all live in the evergreen forests. Wild pigs and deer can be found there, too. In the seas near Italy's shores, fish such as sardines and tuna swim and feed.

A red fox in one of Italy's national parks

9

Men fought each other and beasts for show at the Colosseum in ancient Rome.

Long Ago

People have been living in Italy for thousands of years. Towns and cities grew. In time, the city of Rome became very powerful. The Roman **emperors** controlled many other countries and areas for hundreds of years.

As time went by, other countries wanted the power that Italy had. Slowly, different groups came to Italy and fought over the land. The Roman emperors lost their power and other countries took turns ruling. Spain, Germany, France, and Austria all fought over Italy for hundreds of years.

The first Roman emperor was Augustus.

Italy Today

After years of fighting, even with each other, Italy is peaceful.
The people voted to become a republic in 1946.

Children in Rome read a headline
about Italy's independence in 1946.

Italy now has its own government that makes laws to keep people safe. Like many other countries, Italy's people and government sometimes have problems agreeing on ideas. Even so, Italians are working together to make their country strong.

Italy has also worked to create an organization of countries called the European Union (EU). The EU was formed in 1993, and Italy is a leading member.

Did you know?

The city of Venice was built on islands in a **lagoon**. Seawater usually comes up just below the doorways and people in Venice travel by boats and on bridges. But flooding is a problem, in part because the islands appear to be sinking. Even Piazza San Marco, or St. Mark's Square (above), has flooded. Construction of gates to protect Venice from the sea began in 2003.

13

The People

Italians like to have fun. They also like to work hard at their jobs. Pride in their country—and in their neighborhoods—is important to Italians. They show lots of respect and love to their families and friends. In Italy, loved ones are very important. Visitors to Italy are also treated warmly.

A customer drinks coffee at a café in Italy.

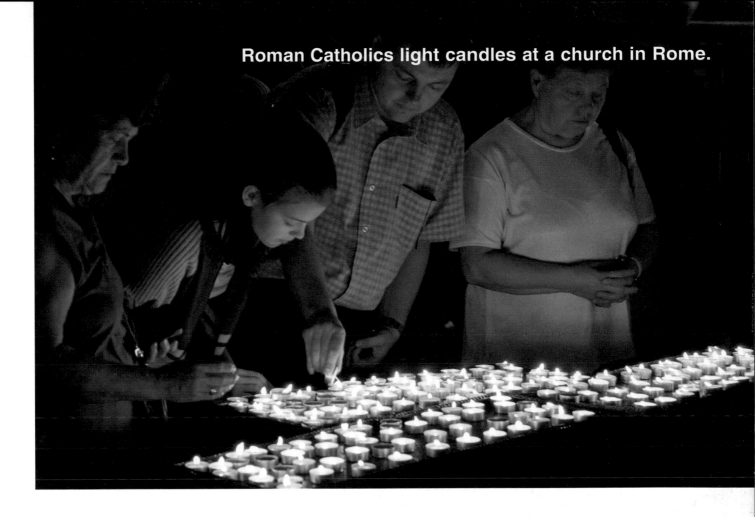

Roman Catholics light candles at a church in Rome.

Most Italians are **Roman Catholics**. Roman Catholics are part of the Christian church led by the pope. Italy is also home to Protestants, Jews, and a growing community of Muslims.

The city of Milan's main shopping area

City Life and Country Life

A shepherd tends his flock on a country road.

More than half of Italy's people live in cities and towns. The big cities have modern structures right next to their historic buildings and museums. You can find shops with the latest fashions, busy street markets, noisy cafés and pizzerias, and crowded train stations. In both cities and towns, most Italians live in apartments.

Life in Italy's countryside is different. People there live a quieter, slower life. There are smaller buildings and narrow roads. In the country, people often walk from place to place. But the cities are often just a train ride away.

Schools and Language

Italian children begin school when they are about six years old. They learn reading, writing, math, and science. Many students have art or music classes, too. When they are a little older, Italian children also learn another language, such as English or French.

Italy's official language is Italian. It is based on an ancient language called Latin. Latin is part of many languages today, even English!

Did you know?

Italy publishes almost 80 daily newspapers.

Italian schoolchildren conduct a science experiment.

A designer uses a computer to model a new Italian motor scooter.

Work

Italy is a busy place, and there are many jobs to do. Some people have jobs in banking, manufacturing, or **technology**. Others work in restaurants, shops, or hotels. Many other Italians work on farms raising crops or animals.

Tourism is an important job in Italy. Tourism is a job where Italians show people from other places about their country. Every year, more and more people are coming to Italy. They want to see and learn about Italy's cities, people, and beautiful land.

Did you **know?**

Most European Union countries, including Italy, use the euro (above). The euro replaced the Italian lira on January 1, 2002.

Food

Italians love to cook and eat. They are known all over the world for their delicious dishes. Pasta is a favorite meal in Italy. It is a thin dough that can be shaped in many different ways. Then it is cooked by boiling it in water.

Did you **know?**

Gelato, a popular treat in Italy, is a soft, rich ice cream with little or no air in it. *Gelato* is Italian for "frozen." It comes in many flavors (below).

An Italian family enjoys an outdoor lunch.

When the pasta is ready, it is mixed with everything from meats to cheeses to thick tomato sauces.

Italians eat many other things, too. Bread, meat, fish, fruit, and vegetables are popular foods. Italians also like to drink wine with their meals. The wine is often made from Italy's own grapes.

Skiing at Courmayeur in Italy

Pastimes

Italians are hard workers, but they like to have fun, too. Skiing, fishing, bicycling, and horse riding are all popular pastimes in Italy. By far, the most important sport for Italians is

Children play soccer in the streets of Naples.

soccer. It is played almost everywhere—from parks and playgrounds to city streets. In fact, soccer is so important to Italians that every big city has its own team.

Spending time with family and friends is very important to Italians. In fact, many people enjoy a *passeggiata* (pah-say-JYAH-tuh) in the evenings. The passeggiata is an evening stroll with loved ones. Families and friends talk and laugh as they walk along the streets and parks.

Holidays

There are lots of different holidays in Italy. Some holidays are huge celebrations for the whole country. Others are small festivals only found in little towns. Many holidays are also celebrated in the United States, such as New Year's Day and Christmas.

A person in costume and mask at the Venice Carnival

Italy is a beautiful country. With such pretty scenery, historic cities, important art treasures, and delicious food, it is sure to be a place you will want to visit!

A girl takes part in a religious festival in Sardinia.

Fast Facts About Italy

Area: 116,305 square miles (301,230 square kilometers)—a little bigger than Arizona

Population: About 58 million people

Capital City: Rome

Other Important Cities: Milan, Naples, Turin, Florence, Genoa, and Venice

Money: The euro. On January 1, 2002, the euro became the only money for daily business in countries that are members of the European Monetary Union.

National Language: Italian. German, French, and Slovene are also spoken in parts of Italy.

National Holiday: Republic Day on June 2 (1946)

Head of Government: The prime minister of Italy

Head of State: The president of Italy

National Flag: The Italian flag has three vertical stripes of green, white, and red.

Famous People:

Christopher Columbus: explorer

Deborah Compagnoni: Olympic skier

Dante: poet

Federico Fellini: film director

Galileo: astronomer and physicist

Leonardo da Vinci: painter and sculptor

Sophia Loren: film actor

Michelangelo: sculptor and painter

Maria Montessori: educator

Luciano Pavarotti: singer

Marco Polo: traveler from 1271 to 1295

Giuseppe Verdi: opera composer

National Song: "Mameli's Hymn" (or *"Inno di Mameli"*) Some people also call the song "Brothers of Italy" (or *"Fratelli d'Italia"*). Goffredo Mameli wrote the words to this song in 1847.

Brothers of Italy,
Italy has arisen,
Has put her head
on the helmet of Scipio.

Where is victory?
Created by God
the slave of Rome.
She crowns you with glory.

Let us unite.
We are ready to die,
We are ready to die.
Italy calls.

Let us unite.
We are ready to die,
We are ready to die.
Italy calls.

(Repeat entire song)

A statue of Romulus, Remus, and the female wolf that rescued them

Italian Legend:

According to legend, infant twin boys named Romulus and Remus were placed in a basket and thrown into the Tiber River. A female wolf rescued them. Years later, the brothers decided to build a city near where the wolf had saved them. Later Romulus killed his brother during a quarrel. Romulus became the first king of the city named after him. And so the city of Rome was founded in 753 B.C.

How Do You Say...

ENGLISH	ITALIAN	HOW TO SAY IT
hello	ciao	CHOW
good-bye	arrivederci	ah-ree-vah-DAYR-chee
please	per favore	PAYR fah-VOH-RAY
thank you	grazie	GRAHTS-yay
one	uno	OO-no
two	due	DOO-ay
three	tre	TRAY
Italy	Italia	ee-TA-leeyah

Glossary

emperors (EM-per-rerz) Emperors are kings. The city of Rome was ruled by emperors long ago.

lagoon (luh-GOON) A lagoon is shallow, quiet water separated from the sea by a strip of land. The city of Venice was built on islands in a lagoon.

peninsula (peh-NIN-soo-luh) A peninsula is a piece of land surrounded by water on almost all sides. Italy is a peninsula.

plains (PLANES) Plains are large, flat areas of land. Italy has many plains.

republic (ri-PUHB-lik) A republic is a form of government that allows the people to vote for their leaders. San Marino is a republic.

Roman Catholics (ROH-muhn KATH-uh-liks) Roman Catholics are members of the Christian church led by the pope. Most Italians are Roman Catholics.

technology (tek-NOL-uh-jee) Technology is the use of science and engineering to do practical things. Some Italians work in the field of technology.

Further Information

Read It

Anderson, Robert. National Geographic. *Countries of the World: Italy.* New York: National Geographic Children's Books, 2006.

De Capua, Sarah. *Italy.* Minneapolis, MN: Compass Point Books, 2003.

Fontes, Justine and Ron. *Italy.* Danbury, CT: Children's Press, 2003.

Look It Up

Visit our Web page for lots of links about Italy:
http://www.childsworld.com/links

Note to Parents, Teachers, and Librarians: We routinely verify our Web links to make sure they are safe, active sites—so encourage your readers to check them out!

Index